Funded by
Alion Science and
Technology

Life Processes

CELLS AND SYSTEMS

Revised and Updated

Holly Wallace

Heinemann Library
Chicago, Illinois

Customer Service 888-454-2279
Visit our website at www.heinemannraintree.com

Designed by David Poole and Kamae Design
Printed in China by WKT Company Limited

10 09 08 07 06
10 9 8 7 6 5 4 3 2 1

New edition ISBN:1-4034-8844-4 (hardcover)
          1-4034-8851-7 (paperback)

The Library of Congress has cataloged the first edition as follows:

Wallace, Holly, 1961- .
      Cells and systems / Holly Wallace.
            p. cm. -- (Life processes)
      Includes bibliographical references (p.) and index.
      ISBN 1-57572-336-0 (library)
        1. Physiology--Juvenile literature. 2. Cells -- Juvenile literature. 3. Tissues -- Juvenile
      e. 4. Organs (Anatomy) -- Juvenile literature. [1. Cells. 2. Organs (Anatomy). 3. Physiology.]
I. Title. II. Series.

QP37 .G333 2000
571--dc21
                        00-040972

Acknowledgments

The publishers would like to thank the following for permission to reproduce photographs:
Action Plus: Glyn Kirk p.**1 5**; Science Photo Library: p.**20**, Andrew Syred pp.**5**, **11**, Eye of Science p.**6**, Claude Nuridsany & Marie Perennou p.**6**, CNRI p.**7**, Dr Jeremy Burgess p.**10**, Manfred Kage p.**1 2**, Prof P Motta/Dept of Anatomy/University La Sapienza/Rome pp.**1 3**, **25**, Profs P Motta, PM Andrews, KR Porter & J Vial p.**1 4**, National Cancer Institute p.**16**, Manfred Kage p.**19**, D Phillips p.**21**, Quest p.**23**, Don Wong p.**24**, Don Fawcett p.**27**, Dr Yorgos Nikas p.**28**, Neil Bromhall p.**28**, L Willatt/East Anglian Genetics Service p.**29**.

Cover photograph of a nerve cell reproduced with permission of Science Photo Library/Steve Gschmeissner.

The publishers would like to thank Mary Jones for her assistance in the preparation of this book.

Disclaimer

CONTENTS

Any words appearing in the text in bold, **like this**, are explained in the glossary.

WHAT ARE CELLS?

All living things are made up of cells. A cell is a tiny unit of living material and is the basic building block of life. Cells are like tiny factories where chemical reactions happen. These reactions keep living things alive and in good working order. Plant and animal cells do similar jobs, such as taking in food, releasing energy, and getting rid of waste. There are some differences, though, in cell structures.

ANIMAL CELLS

An animal cell is like a tiny, jelly-filled bag, held together by a thin, outer skin called a **membrane**. In the center is the **nucleus**, which controls everything that happens inside the cell. The diagram shows the main parts of a typical animal cell.

▼ A typical animal cell.

Cell membrane: the cell's outer "skin," which holds the cell together. It allows food and **oxygen** into the cell and waste products made in the cell out of it.

Cytoplasm: a jelly-like substance that fills most of the cell and is mostly made of **protein** and water. This is where the chemical reactions happen that keep the cell alive.

Nucleus: the control center of the cell. It contains chemical instructions that tell the cell what to do. The nucleus also divides to make new cells for growth, repair, and **reproduction**.

4

PLANT CELLS

Plant cells have all the same features as animal cells but have three extra ones. These are a tough, rigid cell wall made of a substance called **cellulose**, chloroplasts for making food, and a large, permanent vacuole filled with cell **sap**. Here you can see the main parts of a typical plant cell.

▼ A typical plant cell

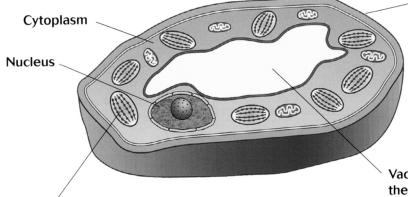

Cytoplasm

Nucleus

Cell wall: a rigid wall around the outside of the cell. It is made of tough fibers of cellulose that support the cell and give it its shape.

Chloroplasts: tiny structures that give plants their green color. They contain a green chemical called **chlorophyll**, which plants use to help them make their own food.

Vacuole: a large space inside the cell that is filled with cell sap. This is a watery fluid containing dissolved **minerals** and food.

HOW MANY CELLS?

Some living things, such as human beings and trees, are made up of millions of cells. They are called multi-cellular, or many-celled, **organisms**. Other living things consist of only one cell. They are called uni-cellular, or single-celled, organisms. The amoeba is a tiny, uni-cellular organism that lives in water. Its cytoplasm flows along to make it move and it feeds by engulfing its prey. To reproduce, an amoeba simply divides in two.

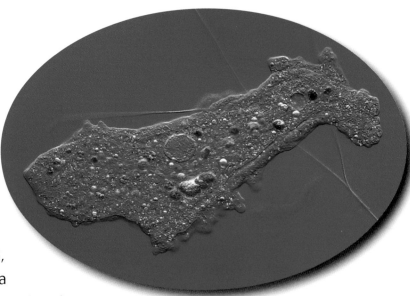

▲ An amoeba is a uni-cellular organism.

CELL SPECIALISTS

Cells make up every part of a living thing, but not all cells look the same. You are made up of many different types of cells. For example, the cells that make your bones, nerves, or muscles, have special features to help them do a particular job. Cells do not work on their own, but are grouped together to build the different parts of your body.

SPECIALIZED CELLS

Cells come in different shapes and sizes, depending on the job they do. They are called "specialized," which means that they can only carry out one type of work. Here are some examples of specialized cells:

- Nerve cells: Nerve cells, or **neurons**, have long, thin fibers for carrying messages all over your body (see page 27).
- Red blood cells: Red blood cells carry oxygen around your body. They are doughnut shaped to give a large surface area for picking up oxygen as quickly as possible (see page 16).
- Ciliated epithelial cells: Cells that form a thin layer to line your air passages. They are covered in tiny hairs called **cilia** that trap harmful dirt and germs (see page 21).
- Root hair cells: A plant's roots take up vital water and minerals from the ground. Near the tips of the roots, there are many long, hair-like cells that provide a large surface area for taking in water.

▲ Tiny cells called cilia line your air passages.

CELLS AND SYSTEMS

Groups of specialized cells make tissues, such as your muscle or bone tissue. Groups of different tissues make organs, such as your heart or lungs. A group of organs working together is called a system, such as your digestive system. This is made up of various organs, for example, your intestines and stomach. All the systems work together to form an organism, such as you!

LIFE PROCESSES

The cells in your body work together to keep you alive. They carry out the seven life processes, which are:

1. Movement: All living things can move their bodies.
2. **Respiration**: This is how cells use oxygen to release energy from food.
3. Sensitivity: All living things sense and respond to changes in the outside world.
4. Feeding: All living things need food for energy and growth.
5. Excretion: All living things must get rid of waste products from their bodies.
6. Reproduction: Living things produce young to replace those that die.

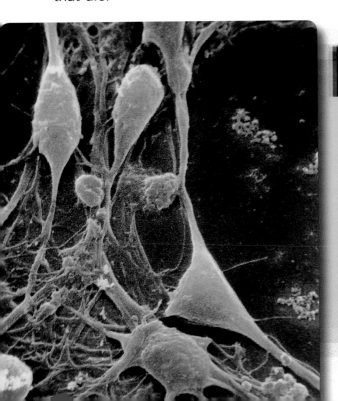

DID YOU KNOW ?

throughout your life and others only live for a few days. When they die, they are replaced with new cells. Some of your brain cells will last a lifetime, your bone cells will last for about 30 years, but the cells that line your small intestine only live for two to three days.

◄ Brain cells can last a lifetime.

PLANT SYSTEMS

Plants range from tiny, single-celled **algae** to towering trees, made of many millions of cells. Most plant cells follow the basic pattern shown on page 5, but some are specialized for particular jobs, such as making food, taking in water, or carrying water around the plant. Groups of plant cells work together to form tissues, such as xylem and phloem (explained on pages 10 and 11). Groups of different tissues form organs, such as the plant's roots, stems, and leaves.

PARTS OF A PLANT

Flowering plants range from daisies and grasses to huge horse chestnut trees. These plants look very different from each other but they all have a similar structure.

Leaves: Cells inside the leaves contain chlorophyll, which absorbs sunlight for photosythesis. **Veins** in the leaves carry food and water around the plant.

Flowers: These contain the plant's sex cells for reproduction.

Stem: The stem supports the plant and holds the leaves up to the sunlight. It also carries food and water up and down the plant.

Roots: The roots anchor the plant in the ground and take in water and minerals.

▲ A plant's systems are all basically the same, whether it is a small flower or a huge tree.

Making food

All living things need energy to survive. This energy comes from their food. Green plants make their own food by **photosynthesis**. This takes place in the plant's leaf cells, inside tiny, disc-shaped structures called chloroplasts. The chloroplasts contain a green chemical called chlorophyll. It uses energy from sunlight to turn **carbon dioxide** from the air and water from the ground into a sugary food called **glucose**. In photosynthesis, plants take carbon dioxide from the air and release oxygen as waste.

Respiration

To release energy from the glucose, plants use oxygen from the air. This is called respiration and it happens inside the plant's cells. The plants take in oxygen through their leaves and give off carbon dioxide as waste. Respiration also continues throughout the night when the plant cannot photosynthesize.

Flower functions

Flowers contain a plant's male parts, which produce **pollen** (containing the male sex cells), and female parts, which produce **ovules** (containing the female sex cells). For a new plant to grow, pollen must travel from the male to the female parts. This is called **pollination**. Then the nuclei of the pollen and ovule fuse, or join together, to make a new cell. This is called **fertilization**. The new cell grows into a seed that contains a new plant and a store of food.

Inside a leaf

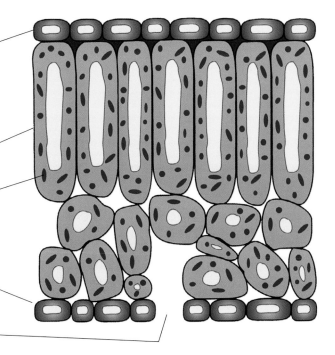

Upper epidermis: This is the upper skin of the leaf. It is made up of a single layer of transparent cells that allow sunlight to pass through to the palisade cells.

Palisade cells: This is a layer of tall, column-like cells that are found just under the upper epidermis where they receive most light.

Chloroplasts: These are found in the cytoplasm of the palisade cells. They contain chlorophyll for photosynthesis.

Lower epidermis: This is the lower skin of the leaf.

Stomata: These are tiny holes in the leaf that allow water and gases in and out (see page 11).

PLANT PLUMBING

Inside a plant, specialized cells work together to carry food and water around the plant in a constant flow. The water is sucked up from the ground through the plant's root system and carried up the stem to the plant's leaves.

ROOT HAIR CELLS

A plant's roots grow downwards and sideways into the ground. Their tips are covered in thousands of tiny, tube-like structures, called root hairs. These are actually formed from the root's outer cells. They grow between the particles of soil and absorb water and minerals. Having so many root hairs greatly increases the roots' surface area so they can take in more water.

▲ The end of a plant's roots are covered in root hairs.

TRANSPORT SYSTEM

From the roots, the water is carried up the plant to the leaves through a system of tiny tubes called xylem. Another set of tubes, called phloem, carry food in the form of sticky sap from the leaves to the rest of the plant. All these tubes form the plant's "plumbing system." The xylem and phloem are arranged in bundles running through the plant's stem, like bundles of tiny drinking straws. Xylem and phloem are called **vascular tissue**. Some simple, non-flowering plants, such as mosses and algae, do not have vascular tissue.

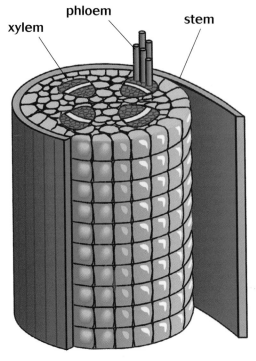

► This is the inside of a plant stem.

WHAT IS OSMOSIS?

Water enters a plant's roots by **osmosis**. This is the way water moves from one cell to another. Some cells contain concentrated cell sap, with a large amount of sugar dissolved in a small amount of water. Others contain much more diluted sap. In osmosis, water moves from the diluted sap to the concentrated sap. Root hairs draw in water by osmosis because their cell sap is stronger than the water in the soil.

LOSING WATER

Some of the water drawn up through the plant is used in photosynthesis. However, most of it is lost through tiny holes on the underside of the leaves. The water then **evaporates** from the leaves into the air. These holes are called stomata. Each stoma (the singular of stomata) is surrounded by two sausage-shaped guard cells (you can see them clearly in the picture), which open and close the stoma.

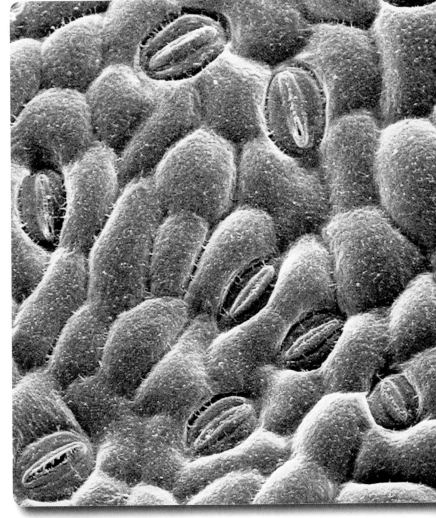

▲ These stomata are on a rose leaf.

11

Bones

Like plants, all animals, including you, are made up of cells. Your body is like a complicated machine, with many different parts. Your cells, tissues, organs, and systems all work together to make you grow and keep you healthy, and to keep your body machine in good working order. Like plant cells, many of the cells in your body, such as those in your skeleton, are specialized to do a particular job.

Skeleton support

Your skeleton is made up of a system of bones inside your body and it has three important jobs to do. First, it acts like the framework of beams and girders inside a building to hold your body up and give it its shape. Without a skeleton, your body would simply collapse in a heap. Second, your skeleton protects the organs of your body from being bumped or knocked. For example, your bony skull protects your delicate brain. Third, your bones anchor your muscles so that you can move around (see page 14).

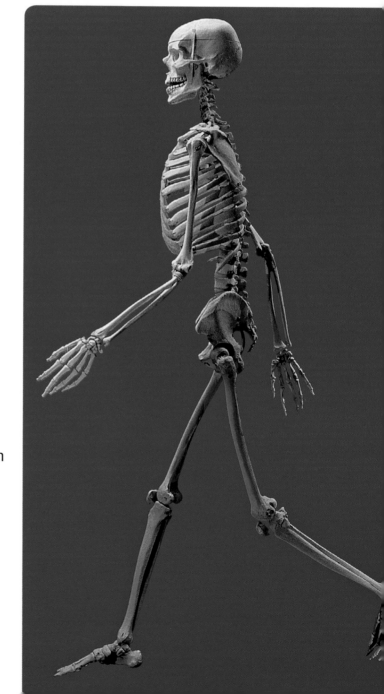

► The human skeleton acts as support and protection for the body.

TOUGH BONES

Bone tissue is highly specialized because of the different jobs it must do. The outer part of a bone is made of tough, non-living tissue. It is mainly minerals, such as **calcium**. It is extremely strong for supporting your body weight and absorbing bumps and knocks. The inside of the bone is living tissue that is soft and spongy. This makes bones light so that you can move about, and flexible so that they do not snap or break too easily. In old age, people's bones have less living tissue so they become brittle and are more easily broken.

Some of the larger bones in your body contain a soft tissue called **marrow**. This makes your red blood cells (see page 16).

GROWING BONES

There are more than 200 bones in your skeleton. They come in a wide range of shapes and sizes, but they all have the same basic structure. When you were a baby, some of your cells formed tough, gristly **cartilage**. Gradually, the cartilage "ossified," or turned into hard bone. This process will carry on until you are about 25 years old. Some of the cartilage never turns to bone. You can still feel cartilage, for example, in the end of your nose and in your ears.

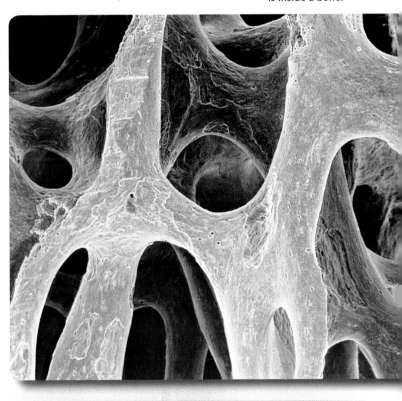

▼ This spongy tissue is inside a bone.

DID YOU KNOW ?

Your bones are covered in a thin, tough, outer layer of living bone cells called the periosteum. If you break a bone, cells in the periosteum divide and multiply, and grow over the break, joining the broken parts together. You might need a cast to help the bones heal straight.

MOVING MUSCLES

There are hundreds of muscles all over your body—in your organs, such as your heart and bladder, or attached between your bones to allow you to move. Your muscles are a type of tissue. The muscles that cover your skeleton are known as stripy muscles because they look stripy under a microscope. The muscles in your organs are called smooth muscles. Smooth muscles work all the time, automatically. They are what make you breathe. A special muscle called the **cardiac** muscle keeps your heart beating.

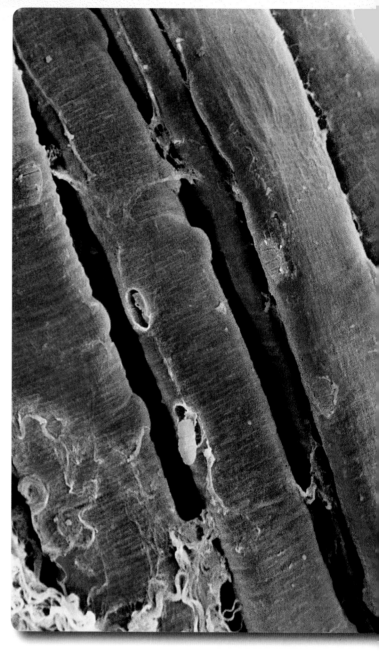

▲ These are stripy muscle fibers.

MUSCLE CELLS

Stripy muscle tissue is made up of bundles of long, thin, thread-like cells, which are usually called muscle fibers. There are more than 2,000 fibers inside a large muscle. Each fiber is made up of finer threads, called myofibrils. Muscle fibers can be up to 11 inches (30 centimeters) long. Their long, thin shape allows them to stretch so that you can move the different parts of your body.

HOW MUSCLES WORK

Muscles are attached to your bones by strong straps called **tendons**. Muscles pull on your bones to make them move. When you want to move your arm, for example, your brain sends electrical signals to your muscles, telling the fibers to contract, or become shorter. This gives a pulling force. Muscles can only pull, not push, so most of your muscles work in pairs. In your upper arm, for example, the biceps muscle contracts to bend your elbow. Then it relaxes and its partner, the triceps, contracts to straighten your arm.

► The stripy muscles of a sprinter are clearly defined.

MUSCLE POWER

Your muscles need a constant supply of oxygen and energy from food to keep them working properly. These are carried to your muscles in your blood, through tiny blood vessels that are wrapped around each bundle of muscle fibers. If supplies of oxygen and energy run low but your muscles are still working hard, they may go into a painful spasm. This is known as a cramp.

DID YOU KNOW ?

You have more than 600 muscles in your body. The largest are in your thighs and backside and are called the gluteus maximus muscles. Your smallest muscles are attached to the tiny bones deep inside your ears. They are called the stapedius muscles and are about the size of a pinhead.

THE CIRCULATORY SYSTEM

Your cells need energy from food as well as oxygen from the air to keep them working properly. These are carried around your body by your blood through blood vessels. Your blood also collects waste products for disposal. Pumped along by your heart, your blood circulates continuously around your body. Your heart, blood, and blood vessels make up your circulatory system.

BLOOD CELLS

Blood is made up of a clear, straw-colored liquid called plasma. Floating in it are red blood cells, white blood cells, and platelets. You have about one gallon (five liters) of blood.

- Plasma is made up of water in which proteins, salts, food, and waste materials are dissolved.

- Red blood cells carry oxygen from your lungs. They are made in the jelly-like marrow inside your large bones. Red blood cells contain a chemical called **hemoglobin**. This is what makes blood red. It absorbs oxygen in your lungs. Your blood then flows to your heart to be pumped around your body.

- White blood cells help your body fight disease. Some eat up harmful germs, which enter your body through cuts, food, or in the air. Others make chemicals called **antibodies**. They stick on to germs and kill them.

- Platelets are tiny fragments of cells that have broken off from larger cells in the bone marrow. They help your blood clot so that you do not lose too much when you cut yourself.

BLOOD VESSELS

Blood travels in tubes called blood vessels. You have so many of these that, put end to end, they would stretch more than twice around the Earth. **Arteries** are strong, muscular tubes that carry blood from your heart. They divide into tiny capillaries that reach your body cells. The walls of the **capillaries** are only one cell thick so that substances can easily pass between them and your cells. The capillaries join up again to form veins, which return the blood to your heart.

▼ This diagram shows the human circulatory system.

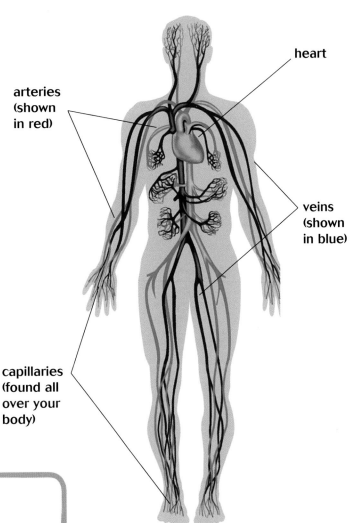

heart

arteries
(shown
in red)

veins
(shown
in blue)

capillaries
(found all
over your
body)

THE HEART

Your heart is an organ. It works like a pump, pushing blood around your body. It pumps, or beats, about once every second and, with each beat, sends blood surging along the arteries. Your heart is made up of strong cardiac muscle. As the muscle contracts, it squeezes blood out and around your body. Each contraction is called a heartbeat. During exercise, your heart has to beat faster to supply your muscles with extra energy. Your **pulse** rate measures how often your heart beats per minute.

DID YOU KNOW ?

A pin-prick of blood contains an amazing 2.5 million red blood cells, 5,000 white blood cells, and 250,000 platelets. In total, you have about 30 billion red blood cells in your body, more than any other type of cell.

THE DIGESTIVE SYSTEM

Everything you do uses energy. Walking and running use lots of energy. Breathing, blinking, and even standing still use energy too. You get this energy from the food you eat. Food also supplies all the chemicals you need for growth and to keep your body working properly. The useful parts of food are carried to your cells by your blood. Only tiny **molecules** of food can pass into your blood, however, so the food must first be broken down. This happens as it passes through your body and travels along your digestive system. This is called **digestion**.

DIGESTING A MEAL

1. Your teeth and tongue chew and crush your food. The food is mixed with **saliva** so it is easier to swallow.

2. The food goes down your **esophagus** into your stomach. It is pushed along by the smooth muscles of the esophagus walls.

3. In your stomach, the food is mixed with digestive juices that contain special **enzymes**. It forms a creamy mixture.

4. The food passes into the first part of your small intestine. A green liquid, called **bile**, that is made in your liver breaks down any fat into tiny droplets. Other enzymes, made in your **pancreas**, break down the food even more.

5. In the second part of the small intestine, called the ileum, the digested food is absorbed into your blood.

6. Any undigested food goes into your large intestine and is passed out of your body as solid waste called **feces**.

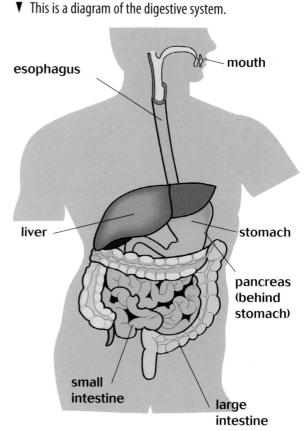

▼ This is a diagram of the digestive system.

mouth

esophagus

liver

stomach

pancreas (behind stomach)

small intestine

large intestine

HOW FOOD GETS INTO YOUR BLOOD

The inner wall of the ileum is covered in tiny, finger-like structures called villi. These make a huge surface area for absorbing food. The villi walls are only one cell thick so that food can pass easily through them and into tiny blood vessels that carry the food around your body to your cells.

► Finger-like villi cover the wall of the small intestine.

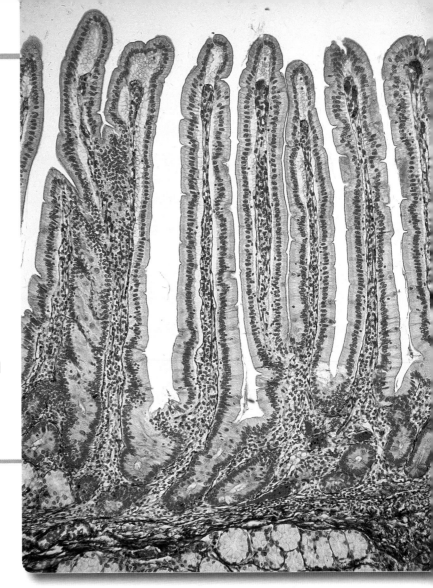

SPEEDY ENZYMES

Enzymes are special chemicals made in your cells. They are called catalysts, which means that they can speed up the chemical reactions taking place in your body. There are thousands of different types of enzymes. Digestive enzymes help break down and dissolve your food as it passes through your digestive system.

DID YOU KNOW ?

Your digestive system is about 30 feet (9 meters) long. A meal takes about three days to pass through. Your small intestine alone measures about 20 feet (6 meters) long. It is only called "small" because it is not very wide.

THE RESPIRATORY SYSTEM

Your body needs oxygen to release the energy from food. When you breathe in, you take air into your lungs. Here the oxygen is removed and carried to all the cells in your body by your blood. Inside the cells, oxygen is used to release energy from food to keep your cells alive and working. Waste carbon dioxide and water are made by your cells. These leave your body when you breathe out. This whole process is called respiration. It is easy to confuse respiration with breathing, but breathing is only part of the whole process of respiration. It describes the first action, when you take air into your lungs, and the last action, when you breathe carbon dioxide out of them.

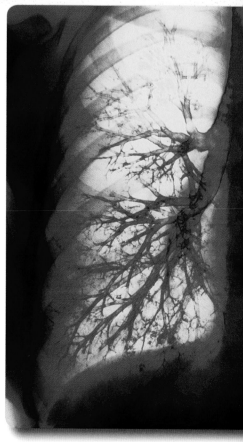

▲ This is the inside of a healthy lung.

BREATHING IN

When you breathe in, air is sucked in through your nose or mouth. It goes down a large tube called the **trachea** and into two tubes called bronchi that lead into your lungs. The bronchi gradually divide to form a network of tiny tubes, called the bronchioles, like the branches of a tree. As you breathe in, your chest muscles move up and out to let your chest expand so that your lungs can fill with air.

▼ This shows the respiratory system.

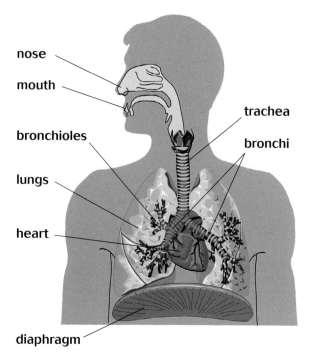

nose
mouth
bronchioles
lungs
heart
trachea
bronchi
diaphragm

GAS EXCHANGE

At the end of the smallest branches are bunches of tiny air sacs called alveoli. When you breathe in, these fill with air, like tiny balloons. The alveoli are covered with very fine blood vessels. In some spots, their walls are only one cell thick. Oxygen from the air passes through the walls and into your blood. Then it is carried around your body to your cells where it is used to release energy. You have millions of alveoli in each lung, giving a huge surface area for absorbing oxygen from the air you breathe.

BREATHING OUT

Your blood also carries waste carbon dioxide from your cells to your lungs to be breathed out. It passes from the blood through the walls of the alveoli and into your lungs. Then it is drawn up through your bronchi and trachea, and out through your nose or mouth. When you breathe out, your chest muscles relax. This lowers your chest and raises your **diaphragm**. This reduces the space in your chest, forcing the air out of your lungs.

▲ The alveoli inside a lung are like tiny air sacs.

DID YOU KNOW ?

Two special types of cells line your air passages. One type is covered in tiny hairs called cilia. The other produces slimy **mucus**. Dust and germs stick to the mucus, and then the cilia "beat" it to the back of your mouth so that you can swallow it and clear the germs away. People who smoke often suffer from painful breathing diseases such as **bronchitis**. This is because the chemicals in cigarette smoke prevent the cilia from doing their job properly.

WATER AND WASTE

Some of the chemical processes happening in your cells make waste products, such as carbon dioxide. We have waste products in our digestive system too, from any food that was undigested. We also have more water in our bodies than we need. All of these must be removed from your body so that they do not harm your cells. You breathe out carbon dioxide (see page 21) during respiration, and get rid of waste food as feces (see page 18). You lose waste water when you **urinate**. Your body is about two-thirds water, and it needs to stay that way for your cells to function properly. If you take in more water than you need, your kidneys make **urine** to get rid of the liquid and other waste products.

THE URINARY SYSTEM

Your kidneys and bladder are known as your urinary system because they make and store urine. Your two kidneys are in your lower back, level with your waist. As blood passes through them, the kidneys filter out waste water and other substances. This waste liquid is called urine. It flows down two tubes, called ureters, into your bladder, an organ that is like a stretchy, muscular bag. The urine is stored in your bladder until you go to the bathroom. Then it passes out of your body through a long tube called the urethra.

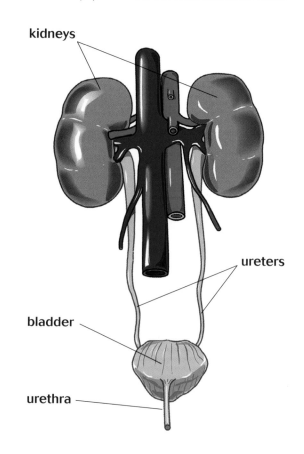

▼ The urinary system filters out waste and excess water.

kidneys

ureters

bladder

urethra

In your lifetime, you will make about 10,500 gallons (40,000 liters) of urine. This is enough to fill about 200 bathtubs! Each day, your kidneys process about 40 gallons (150 liters) of liquid. But most of this is cleaned and goes back into your blood.

FILTER SYSTEM

Each kidney contains over a million tiny filtering units called nephrons. Blood flows into your kidneys through your **renal** artery. When it has been cleaned, the blood flows out through your renal vein and continues to circulate around your body.

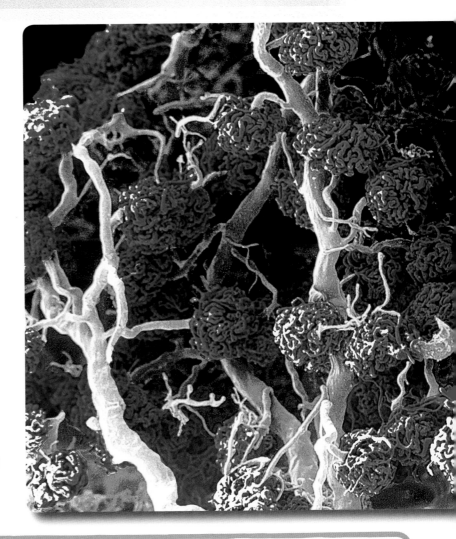

► The tiny filters inside a kidney are called nephrons.

POISON CONTROL

Your liver is the largest organ in your body, weighing more than 3 pounds (1.5 kilograms). It does several very important jobs. When your blood has absorbed digested food, it makes a detour through your liver. Your liver stores some of the **nutrients** in the food and changes others into more useful forms. It also gets rid of the toxic, or poisonous, substances found in some food and drink, by turning them into harmless substances. This process is called detoxification.

YOUR SENSES

Your five senses are sight, hearing, smell, taste, and touch. They tell you about the outside world. You receive information through special **sensory** nerve cells called **receptors**. They react to changes in light or sound, for example, and send messages to your brain. There, the information is processed and your brain tells you what is happening. Many receptors are grouped to form sense organs, such as your eyes, ears, or nose.

EYES AND SEEING

You see things because light from an object enters your eyes. It is focused by the cornea and lens (see diagram below) to project a sharp, upside-down image on to the retina. Millions of light-sensitive cells on the retina react to the light and send messages to your brain. It interprets the signals and produces the picture you see.

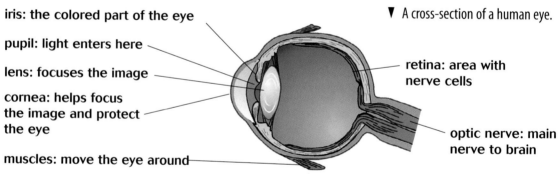

iris: the colored part of the eye

pupil: light enters here

lens: focuses the image

cornea: helps focus the image and protect the eye

muscles: move the eye around

▼ A cross-section of a human eye.

retina: area with nerve cells

optic nerve: main nerve to brain

DID YOU KNOW ?

The light-sensitive receptor cells in the retinas of your eyes are called rods and cones. You have about 120 million rods and 7 million cones in each eye. Rods detect black and white, and light intensity. Cones detect colors. Some people are color blind and cannot see certain colors properly because they have faulty cone cells.

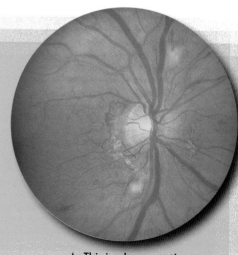

▲ This is a human retina.

EARS AND HEARING

Sounds are vibrations, or waves, in the air. Your ears funnel them down your ear canal to the eardrum. This is a thin membrane that vibrates as the sound waves hit it. The vibrations are passed on to three tiny bones, then on to another membrane, and then to the **cochlea**. This is filled with liquid that also vibrates. Special nerve cells detect the vibrations and turn them into signals, which travel to your brain. Here they are turned into the sounds that you hear.

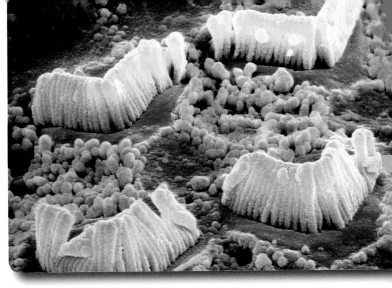

▲ These are sound-sensitive cells inside an ear.

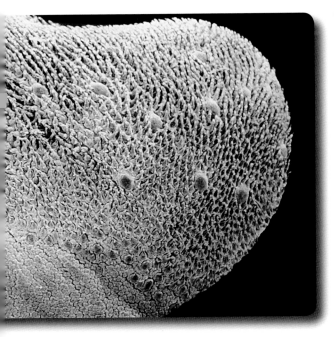

TASTE AND SMELL

Your tongue and nose are your organs of taste and smell. Your tongue is covered in taste buds (left), which are lined with taste-sensitive cells. They can detect four main tastes—sweet, salty, sour, and bitter. Smells are chemicals floating in the air. They travel up your nose and are picked up by smell receptor cells. Taste and smell are closely linked. If you have a cold and your nose is blocked, you may find it difficult to taste your food.

SKIN AND TOUCH

Millions of sense receptors are packed beneath the surface of your skin and each type detects a different sensation. Some are sensitive to touch, temperature, and pressure. Some tell you if the things you feel are rough, smooth, hard, or soft. Other receptors detect pain, which warns you that something is wrong with your body.

Nervous System

Your brain, nerves, and **spinal cord** form your body's central nervous system. This processes the information your senses receive about the outside world, and instructs your body how to think, feel, or react. Your nerves are like long, fine wires, carrying messages in the form of electrical signals between your brain and other parts of your body. Your spinal cord acts as the main pathway for these messages to travel along. Your nerves branch out from it to carry the messages all over your body.

Your amazing brain

Your brain controls every part of your body, and everything that you think, learn, remember, and feel. It has up to 10 billion nerve cells, or neurons. Nerves carry information about the outside world from your senses to your brain, where it is sorted and processed. Then your brain sends messages along your nerves to your body to tell you what action, if any, to take.

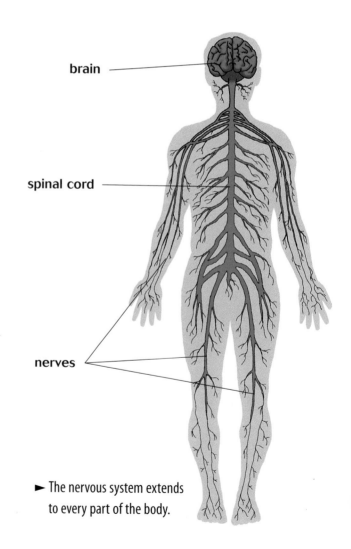

brain

spinal cord

nerves

► The nervous system extends to every part of the body.

NERVE CELLS

A nerve is made up of bunches of long fibers, called axons, which run from the cell bodies of the neurons. Shorter fibers, called dendrites, also branch off from the cell bodies. You have a vast network of about 100 billion neurons running throughout your body. There are two main types of neurons. Sensory neurons carry messages from your sensory organs (see pages 24 to 25) to your central nervous system. **Motor neurons** carry messages from your central nervous system to your muscles to make them move.

HOW NERVES WORK

One neuron's axons lie very close to the next neuron's dendrites, but they do not actually touch. Nerve signals pass from one neuron to another by "jumping" over a tiny gap called a synapse. To cross the gap, the signals must change from electrical signals into chemicals called neurotransmitters. Once they have crossed, they turn back into electrical signals again. One neuron has synapses with many other neurons. This means that it can receive many different electrical signals.

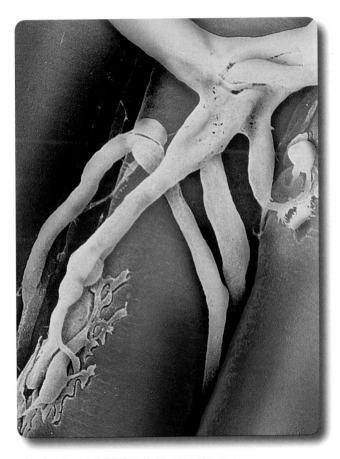

► This is a synapse, or nerve junction.

REPRODUCTION

Reproduction means the creation of new life. Human beings reproduce sexually, which means that there are two parents who each make sex cells. Male sex cells are called sperm. Female sex cells are called eggs. For a baby to develop, a sperm must join with an egg to form a new cell. This is called fertilization.

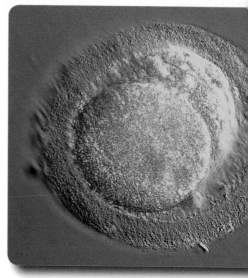

▲ This hows the first cell division of a fertilized egg.

REPRODUCTIVE SYSTEMS

Your reproductive system starts working at **puberty**. This usually begins at the age of 11–13 for girls and 12–14 for boys. An egg is made ready in one of a female's two **ovaries**. It then travels down a tube, called the Fallopian tube. If it meets a sperm cell, it may be fertilized. Sperm cells are made in a male's **testes**. They swim along two tiny tubes, called sperm ducts, to his **penis**.

MALE AND FEMALE

A baby develops when a sperm meets and joins with an egg in the female's body. This happens when a male and female have sexual intercourse. After fertilization, the two cells make one new cell. This begins to divide until it forms a ball of cells. Then it embeds itself in the female's uterus (womb). Over the next nine months, it grows and develops into a baby.

CELL INSTRUCTIONS

Each sex cell carries instructions called genes. Genes are like chemical codes that say what a living thing is and what it looks like. They determine the characteristics you inherit from your parents, such as hair and eye color. They are carried on very fine threads of material, called chromosomes, inside the nuclei of your cells. You inherit 23 chromosomes from each parent. The chromosomes that determine your sex are X and Y chromosomes. All eggs carry X chromosomes. Half the sperm carry X chromosomes and half carry Y. If two X chromosomes join, the baby will be a girl. If an X and a Y chromosome join, the baby will be a boy.

CELL DIVISION

For a living thing to grow bigger, new cells must be made. Most cells reproduce by splitting in two. There are two types of cell division:

- Mitosis: The nucleus splits in two, forming two new daughter cells. Each of these cells has a full set of chromosomes. The two cells are identical. This type of division is used for growth and repair.
- Meiosis: The nucleus splits in two, forming two new daughter cells. Each of these cells has only half the total number of chromosomes of its parent cell. The two cells are not identical. This type of division is used to produce sex cells for reproduction.

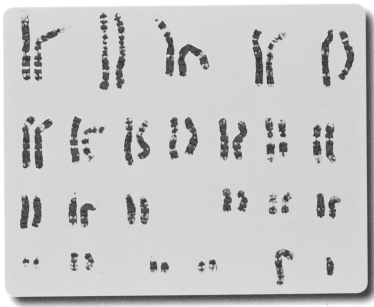

▲ These are male chromosomes.

GLOSSARY

algae   very simple plants found in both salt water and fresh water

antibody   chemical made by some types of white blood cells. Antibodies stick on to germs and kill them.

artery   blood vessel that carries blood away from your heart

bile   thick green liquid made in your liver that breaks down fats in your food

bronchitis   chest infection that makes breathing difficult and painful

calcium   mineral that is essential for building your bones

capillary   smallest blood vessel

carbon dioxide   gas that living things breathe out as waste during respiration. Plants use carbon dioxide in photosynthesis.

cardiac   to do with the heart

cartilage   rubbery, flexible tissue

cellulose   tough material made of fibers found in plant cell walls

chlorophyll   green pigment (coloring) found inside plant cells that absorbs energy from sunlight for use in photosynthesis

cilia   tiny hair-like structures that cover some cells

cochlea   curled tube, filled with liquid, in the inner ear. Sound waves shake the liquid, which pulls on nerve endings to send signals to the brain.

cytoplasm   jelly-like substance that fills cells

diaphragm   muscle under your chest that contracts and relaxes so you can breathe in and out

digestion   way in which food is broken down and processed as it passes through your body

enzyme   chemical made in your cells. Some enzymes help break down your food during digestion.

esophagus   large tube in your throat through which you swallow food (also called the gullet)

evaporate   when a liquid, such as water, turns into gas

feces   solid waste you pass when you go to the bathroom

fertilization   joining together of a male and female sex cell to produce a new living thing

glucose   simple sugar

hemoglobin   chemical in your blood that makes it look red and carries oxygen around your body

marrow   jelly-like substance inside some of your larger bones that makes new red and white blood cells

membrane   thin sheet of tissue

mineral   substance that helps build your body and keep it healthy

molecule   tiny particle of a substance

motor neurons   nerve cells that carry messages from your brain to your muscles

mucus   slimy substance that helps protect the lining of your nose, lungs, and stomach

neuron   nerve cell

nucleus   rounded structure inside a cell that is the cell's control center. Nuclei is the plural of nucleus.

nutrient   substance in food that your body needs in order to function

organism   scientific word for living thing

osmosis   way in which fluid passes from one cell to another

ovary   part of a female's reproductive system. The two ovaries make egg cells.

ovule   structures containing the female sex cells of a plant; after fertilization, they become seeds

oxygen   gas that living things use in respiration

pancreas   group of cells (organ) that is part of your digestive system. The pancreas makes enzymes that help break down your food.

penis   part of a male's reproductive system. During sexual intercourse, sperm cells swim down the penis into the female's body.

photosynthesis process by which green plants make their own food from carbon dioxide and water, using energy from sunlight absorbed by their chlorophyll

pollen tiny grains that contain the male sex cells of plants

pollination transfer of pollen from a male flower to a female flower, or from male to female parts of a flower

protein chemical substance that living things use for growth

puberty time in a girl or boy's life when their bodies change from being a child to being an adult

pulse beats of your heart; you can feel a pulse in your wrist or neck

receptor special nerve cell that senses the outside world and sends messages about it to your brain

renal to do with the kidneys

reproduction creation of new life

respiration way that energy is released from food, using oxygen

saliva liquid made in your mouth that helps break down your food

sap liquid inside a plant that carries food and water

sensory sensory neurons are nerve cells that carry messages from your sense organs to your brain

spinal cord thick bundle of nerves running down your back, inside your spine or backbone

tendon thick strap of tissue that connects muscle to bone

testes part of a male's reproductive system where sperm cells are made

trachea long tube running down your throat used in breathing (also called the windpipe)

urinate to pass urine when you go to the bathroom

urine liquid you pass out of your body that contains excess water and other waste substances

vascular tissue system that carries sap around a plant (made of xylem and phloem)

vein 1) tiny tube in a leaf that carries food and water 2) vessel that carries blood back to your heart

FIND OUT MORE

Internet research

You can find out more about cells and systems on the Internet. Use a search engine such as www.google.com or www.yahooligans.com to search for information. A search for "cells and systems" will bring back lots of results but it may be difficult to find the information you want. Try refining your search to look for some of the specific systems or ideas mentioned in this book, such as "human muscles" or "the circulatory system."

More books to read

Morgan, Sally. *Cells and Cell Function*. Chicago: Heinemann Library, 2006.

Parker, Steve. *The Brain and Nervous System*. Chicago: Heinemann-Raintree, 2004.

Riley, Peter. *Making Sense of Science*. Mankato, Minn.: Smart Apple Media, 2005.

INDEX